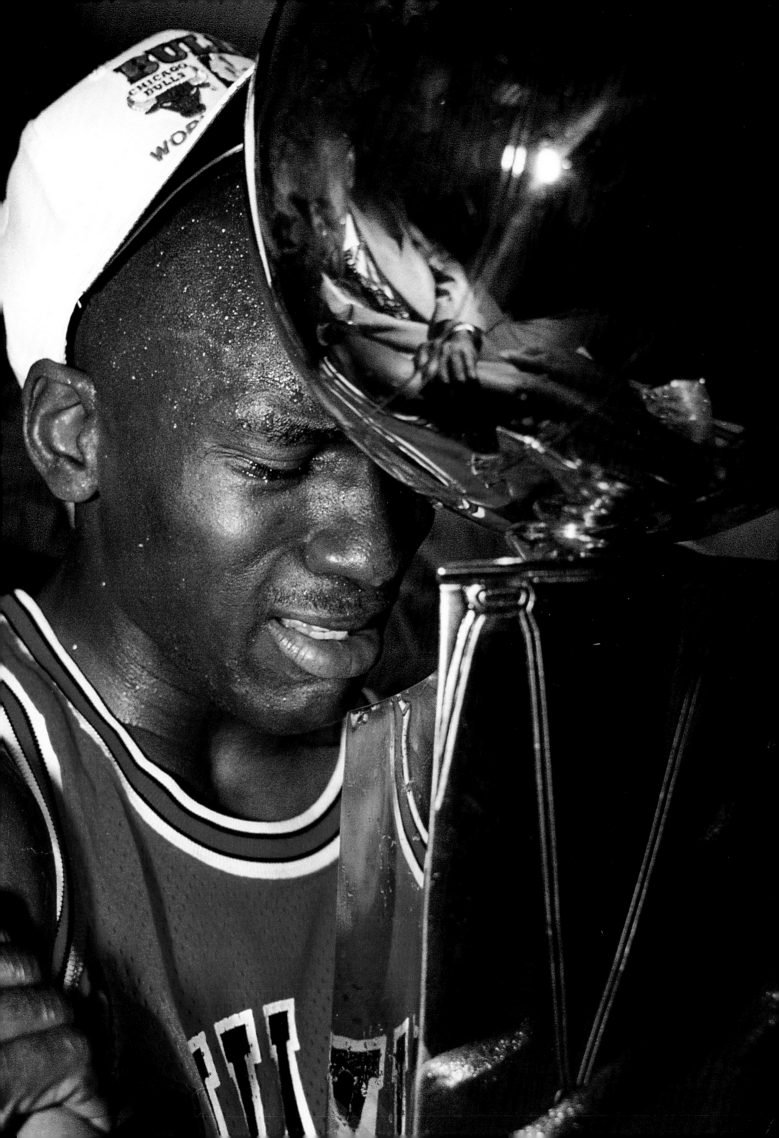

Memories of Mike

PRESENTED BY BECKETT PUBLICATIONS

The First Shot

March 29, 1982, NCAA title game

Memories of Mike

Copyright© 1999 by Dr. James Beckett
All rights reserved under International and Pan-American Copyright Conventions.

Published by: Beckett Publications
15850 Dallas Parkway
Dallas, TX 75248

ISBN: 1-887432-67-1

First Edition: March 1999
Designer: Matthew Klug

Beckett Corporate Sales and Information (972) 991-6657

A book dedicated to the basketball career of Michael Jordan can be, well, like the man himself, overwhelming. Trying to put it all into perspective can be like trying to guard Mike, which, for opponents in high school, college and 13 NBA seasons, was, in a word, impossible.

Thank goodness for Bob Costas. As an NBC broadcaster covering Jordan, it was his job not to be overwhelmed by the phenomenal player and his larger-than-life presence. An expert observer, his memories of Mike accomplish the rare feat of stopping Jordan, of freezing in time his soaring legend just long enough for us to appreciate the reasons for his unmatched popularity and his rarefied place in NBA history.

COSTAS ON STYLE

"The fact that he has been beautiful to watch adds to his status. Jordan, because of what he's done and how he's carried himself and how he's looked doing it, has (generated an) enormous amount of good will that protects him from the few things that might be less attractive or that might deserve criticism.

"For example, there's nothing appealing about the way he speaks about (Bulls GM) Jerry Krause, like a high school bully ridiculing the fat kid in the back of the bus. And what kind of crazy deal is it to say that you are hurt beyond forgiveness when someone who hands you $30 million says, perhaps kiddingly, 'Some day I may regret this.' Yet I still would hold Michael Jordan up as an example of greatness and dignity in many respects. You could do a whole lot worse than saying, 'This is a guy I admire.' "

COSTAS ON GREATNESS

"Michael Jordan is, simultaneously, the greatest player who has ever played in the NBA and the most overrated. Because, with television being what it is, and the modern American's attention span being what it is, and hype and marketing being what they are, historical perspective is all but completely lost.

Do I think he's the best who ever played? Yes I do. Do I think he's twice as good as Magic Johnson? Or disproportionately better than Larry Bird? Or, in his context and in his time, that much better than Oscar Robertson? Or Wilt Chamberlain or Bill Russell? Nope.

"Also, are the Bulls among the best teams of all time? Of course they are. Would they have won championships in any decade? Of course they would. But I don't think they would have won six. Television, including NBC, is culpable in this, too. It's in the best interest of anybody who is selling something, whether it's a Michael Jordan lunch box or the next telecast, for it to be true that (Chicago) is the best team of all time and (Jordan) is the best player of all time.

"You can't take anything away from him. If I were forced, with a gun at my head, to pick the best basketball player of all time, I would pick Michael Jordan. If somebody else were to pick Chamberlain or Bird, I could happily argue Jordan's case and prove that the other guy was wrong.

"Still, proportionately, (the hype) is all out of whack."

CONTENTS

chapter one
Memorable Moments 10

chapter two
Greatest Games 32

chapter three
Refuse to Lose 54

chapter four
Invaluable Commodity 76

chapter five
Reflections of Greatness 98

CHAPTER 1

Memorable Moments

So many memorable moves, so many memorable shots, so little time on the 24-second clock . . .

Chicago, 1988 Slam-Dunk contest. In need of something to bring the house down, Jordan borrows a page out of the Julius Erving flight manual. Air Jordan motors down the runway, lifts off at the free throw line, soars through the air, throws down a tomahawk dunk and steals the crown from Atlanta's Dominique Wilkins.

Cleveland, Game 5, 1989 Eastern Conference quarterfinals. The Cavaliers are just seconds away from the series clincher when Jordan grabs the in-bounds pass, dribbles to the free throw line and hangs in the air for what seems to be, oh, 23 seconds. While poor Craig Ehlo sails past him, Jordan drains a straight-away 18-footer and earns a spot next to John Elway and Art Modell on the city's list of most-hated.

Chicago, Game 2, 1991 NBA Finals. Jordan elevates to the right of the bucket, where he is challenged by Los Angeles defender Sam Perkins. In a split-second of mid-air magic, he switches the rock to his left hand, then kisses the ball in off the glass. Darn if thousands of jaws hit the floor before Jordan does.

Chicago, Game 1, 1992 NBA Finals. After he bags the last of his NBA Finals record six three-pointers against Portland, Jordan does the only thing he can do: spreads his hands and shrugs his shoulders as if to tell the sellout crowd and the national television audience, "I can't help myself." Later he says, "Sometimes I fascinate myself. I can't explain it."

Salt Lake City, Game 6, 1998 NBA Finals. Uncanny instincts, sleight of hand, cold-blooded dramatics – the Best of Michael is there to be seen in one tidy 37-second sequence in the final minute. After John Stockton sinks a three-pointer to give the Jazz an 86-83 advantage with 42 seconds on the clock, Jordan mistakes Bryon Russell for a turnstile, then lays the ball in over Antoine Carr to make it a one-point game. On the next ball possession, the Jazz call on their own go-to guy, Karl Malone, in the low post. It's a strategy that fools no one, least of all Jordan, who promptly sneaks up from behind and relieves the Mailman of the ball. Still, there was some unfinished business at hand. Jordan dribbles nearly three-quarters the length of the court, where he encounters Russell at the top of the key once again. After Jordan makes a move to his right, Russell reaches in for the ball. In a nanosecond, Jordan resorts to one of his favorite moves: karate-chop the defender's lead arm with his non-dribbling hand, a bit of chicanery that he performs so deftly that few ever see it until after the fact. With Russell back on his heels, Jordan has the time and the space to unleash his last ever shot in an NBA game, an 18-footer . . . Nothing but net.

Karl Malone

Utah forward, asked who was best after Jordan won Game 1 in 1997 with a 20-footer

"What do you want me to say, Michael Jordan, like everybody else? Well I think obviously it's Michael Jordan. Whatever Karl Malone says, it doesn't really matter. I think down the stretch Michael wanted the ball in crunch time. He got it, he made it. It's hard to argue with that."

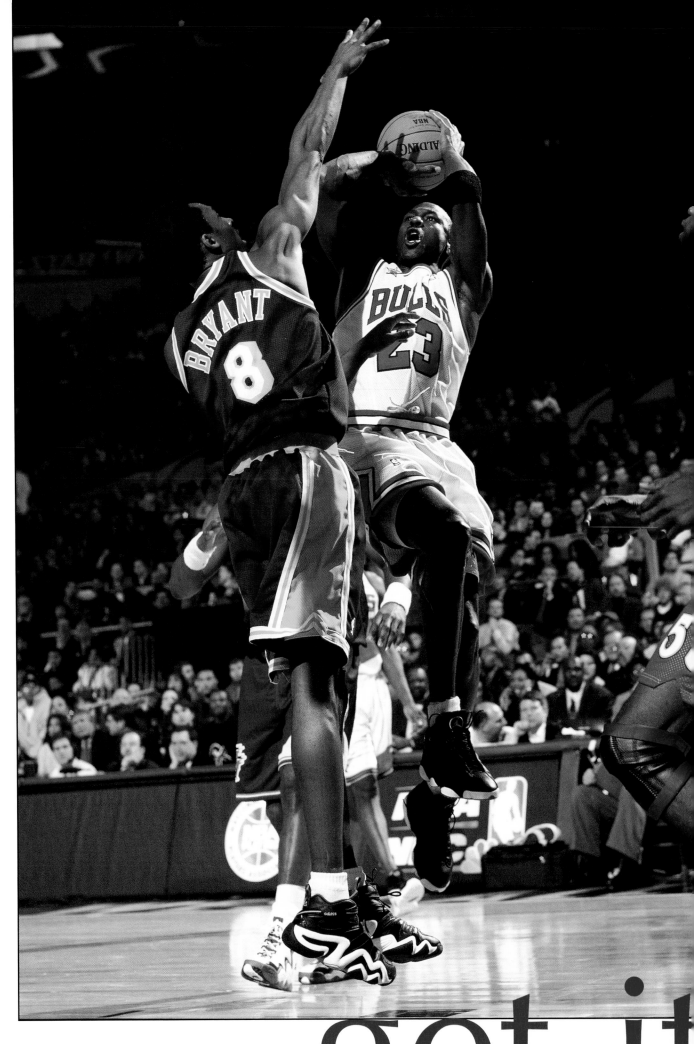

get it

14

Kobe Bryant

Lakers phenom, after his 1-on-1 duel in the 1998 All-Star Game

"All I wanted to do was get a hand up, try to play him hard, try different tactics on him. I can use it for my knowledge in the future. . . . I was like, 'Cool, let's get it on.' "

"I looked over at M.J. and he had this look in his eye like, 'You're right, they're trying to plug this as Kobe going after Michael.' We all took that personal."

Reggie Miller

Pacers star guard on that matchup

Magic Johnson

Lakers great

"My favorite memory of Michael was when we were both on the 1992 Olympic Dream Team in Barcelona. We had a lot of fun playing cards. He won a lot of my money, and I won a lot of his money. But the most memorable play had to be that shot in the '91 Finals when he drove to the basket, soared, levitated, palmed the ball in his right hand to dunk it and then said, 'Wait a minute, I think I'll lay it up with my left hand,' and then he switched hands and laid it in off the glass."

soared

I'm on fire

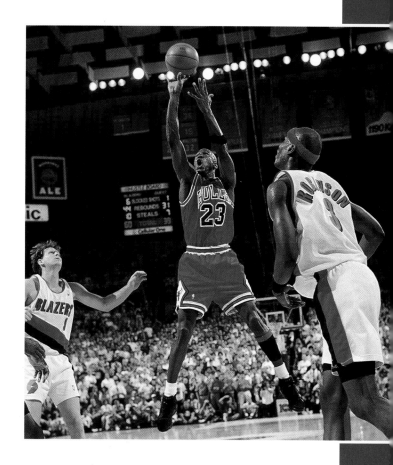

David J. Stern

NBA commissioner on Jordan's famous I-can't-help-myself shrug during his
three-point barrage in Game 1 of the 1992 Finals vs. Portland

"Being at courtside when he hit those shots (a record six three-pointers in the first half against Portland) is a great memory. He turned to Magic (Johnson), who was announcing the game, and shrugged. It could have been in the Finals. It could have been in the schoolyard. It was just a couple of basketball players exchanging a glance. Michael shrugged like he was apologizing and saying, 'Hey, I can't help it. I don't know what's going on. I'm on fire.' It was the most delightful moment, so natural and so wonderful."

Isiah Thomas

former Detroit Pistons All-Star guard

"One of the most exciting memories I have was of a game we played against him in the Silverdome when he dropped 61 points on us (April 16, 1987). Terry Tyler was guarding him and Tyler was known as one of the best leapers in basketball. Jordan was coming down the left side of the court and he took off from way outside the lane and everybody in the Silverdome froze to see this jumping contest. As Tyler jumped, he met Jordan in mid-air. But Jordan went up another two feet, grabbed Tyler by his jersey, carried him to the basket, dunked the basketball and almost threw Tyler on the floor. It was one of those things that make you say, 'Did you see that?' "

dropped 61

Craig Ehlo

Cleveland Cavalier on Jordan's jumper at the buzzer to beat the Cavaliers in Game 5 of their Eastern Conference first-round series on May 7, 1989

"That's something where, when you talk about Cleveland, it's part of the history. Back in 1954 in the World Series, there was The Catch (Willie Mays made his famous catch of Vic Wertz's shot to deep center field). Then they had The Drive, when John Elway led the Broncos back against the Browns (in 1986). And there's The Shot. So I'm part of that Cleveland history, too.

"Three seconds on the clock is definitely an eternity. I'm sure there were guys, the die-hard fans, who said, 'Ehlo should have tripped him, poked him in the eye or even shot him to keep that shot from going in.' I look at the sequence every now and then to see if he really was up in the air longer than I was, because I know we jumped at the same time."

the shot

the shot

the shot

22

Jordan

on the game-winning jumper with 17 seconds remaining
to beat Georgetown in the 1982 NCAA title game

"That is the beginning of my career, all the way around. That shot gave me the confidence that I could compete on a national level with the competition I had to face. "It's frightening to think of how things would have (turned out) if I had missed it."

Ron Coley

then assistant coach at Laney High School (Wilmington, N.C.) where Michael played high school ball

"There was one game at New Bern (N.C.) where a player was really dogging Michael all the way up the court, sticking right on him. Then about a step or two past the foul line, Michael just jumped right over him and slammed one."

don't do this

Charles Barkley

All-Star forward for Philadelphia, Phoenix and Houston

"One of my memories of Michael came in 1989. I switched out on him on a pick-and-roll and I said, 'I got him.' And he stood up, held the ball and said, 'I don't think you want to do this.' And he started laughing. I got in a perfect defensive stance. Then he scored."

Shawn Kemp

Cleveland Cavaliers forward

"The one thing anybody fears when they play against Michael Jordan is getting poster-ized. When I saw all those highlight films of him dunking on people, I swore to myself, 'There's no way I'll ever let him dunk on me like that.' Then he did it. During a game in Chicago when I had a lot of my relatives in the house, Jordan dunked on me right in front of my family. Talk about embarrassing, I was one very embarrassed man."

Jayson Williams

New Jersey forward, after the Bulls' 3-0 sweep of the Nets in 1998

"I remember one play. They'd been driving down the middle so I said I'd take a hard foul on Michael. The next time down, he hit me in the side of the head and said, 'Don't think I forgot about that.' "

out of the way

Steve Kerr

Bulls guard, on Jordan in Game 6 of the 1998 Finals

"When we called timeout and were down three with 45 seconds left, I thought to myself this would be a great chance for a three-pointer to tie the game. I mentioned that to Phil (Jackson), and Phil looked at me with this disgusted look and said, 'Steve, face it, last year was a fluke. Give the ball to Michael and get the hell out of the way.' That's what I did. But for what it's worth, I thought I did a fantastic job of getting out of his way."

CHAPTER 2

Greatest Games

Has Michael Jordan ever played a bad game? Did Bogart ever do a bad movie? Sure, some of them have been better than others, but to pick the best of Michael is to choose between "Casablanca" and "The African Queen." Which is to say, all thumbs up. Start with the afternoon of April 20, 1986, at Boston. As mismatches went, the Bulls of Jawan Oldham, Kyle Macy and Orlando Woolridge versus the Celtics of Larry Bird, Kevin McHale and Robert Parish was supposed to be the NBA playoff version of the St. Valentine's Day Massacre. But nobody informed Jordan, who played just 18 regular season games because of a fractured foot. He scores 63 points and nearly swipes Game 2 single-handedly before his team finally loses in double overtime. "When a coach looks down the bench, he can tell who wants to play by the looks on their faces," recalls then Celtics boss K.C. Jones. "But when I looked for volunteers to play against Jordan that game, there were a lot of heads buried in towels."

Fast forward to the afternoon of May 7, 1989. Richfield Coliseum in suburban Cleveland. Fifth and final game, Eastern Conference quarterfinals. Cavaliers 100, Bulls 99, with time running out. Jordan bags a straight-away 17-footer over Craig Ehlo and the place goes stone-cold silent. Up to this point, the Bulls never had won a playoff series in the Jordan era. Just Did It.

Jump all the way to the night of June 11, 1997, Game 5 of the 1997 NBA Finals at Utah. At 3 o'clock that morning, Jordan was dog sick with the stomach flu, the result of some tainted pizza courtesy of room service. He couldn't sleep. He couldn't eat. By halftime, he is dehydrated. In the third quarter, Jordan appears ready to be administered the Last Rites, but not before he scores 38 points and wills a two-point victory. Two days later, Jordan and Co. administer Last Rites to the Jazz.

Advance one year later to June 14, 1998, Game 6 of the Finals at Utah. It's crunch time, or should we say, Jordan time. In a swan song Hollywood couldn't pull off, Jordan finishes with 45 points and does indeed single-handedly deliver title No. 6 to the Windy City. Even Phil Jackson believes the performance deserves an Oscar. "Last year in the fifth game, I didn't think he could top that," the head coach says. "But tonight he topped it."

Each performance is Academy Award material, but several others deserve mention: the career-high 69 points at Cleveland on March, 28, 1990; the 56 points in the playoff series clincher at Miami on April, 29, 1992; the smooth 64 at Orlando Jan. 16, 1993. Oh yeah, then there's the one at Cleveland on Feb. 9, 1997, when with 14 points, 11 rebounds and 11 assists, he became the first player to record a triple-double in an All-Star Game.

Here's looking at you, Mike.

Larry Bird

"I think he's God disguised as Michael Jordan. He's the most awesome
player in the NBA. Today in Boston Garden, on national TV, in the
playoffs, he put on one of the greatest shows of all time."

he's God

jacked

Doug Collins

after his first game as head coach of the Bulls in 1986, when Jordan exploded for 50 points against the Knicks

"I've never seen anything like Michael Jordan – ever, ever, never. Michael was so jacked up before that game. I could tell in the pregame shootaround. He was clowning around and trying to let out all that nervous energy. Give credit to No. 23. He sets the tone, just like Larry Bird. The thing I've enjoyed most about him is, he just never stops working, and everyone else around him seems to feed off of that."

Steve Kerr

Bulls guard on Game 5 of the 1997 NBA Finals victory over Utah

"The only person who can stop Michael is himself. Even sickness can't. Everybody remembers how sick he was in Game 5 of (the 1997) Finals. They asked me, 'What do you think will happen? Michael's sick.' Michael had a case of food poisoning, stomach flu or something, and I said, 'He'll probably get 40 points.' Well, Michael goes out and scores 38 and we win. Those are terrible expectations to have of a person. I don't envy him at all. I don't know how he does it, but he manages to come up big every time."

come up big

sleeping

Dave Checketts

Madison Square Garden CEO and New York Knicks
top chief, on the 1993 conference playoff series

"The Bulls were ready for us to pass them, but the Atlantic City (gambling scandal spawned by New York newspapers) woke up a sleeping giant. Jordan came out with a vengeance after that, and it all culminated in Game 5 (when Jordan scored a triple-double and the Bulls won, 94-92), which was absolutely heartbreak."

giant

Dikembe Mutombo

Atlanta Hawks center recalling March 27, 1998, when Jordan scored 34 in an 89-74 victory before 62,046 in the Georgia Dome

"I think that tonight the people paid Michael Jordan the highest tribute. I mean, we had 60,000 in this dome tonight and they came for one reason. They came to see Michael Jordan. No other player could draw a crowd like this, and . . . I thank Michael that I will be able to tell my grandchildren that I was part of this. If he never comes back to Atlanta again, this is the best way for him to come his last time."

Steve Kerr

"My favorite (memory) was where he had one of his worst games and we still almost won. We were in Miami playing the Heat a day after Michael had reportedly played 46 holes of golf. Well, Michael missed his first 14 shots and was 2-for-22 after three quarters. It was maybe the worst shooting performance I've ever seen anybody have. But in the fourth quarter, Michael got hot and scored 20 points, including 18 in a row for us and we trimmed what had been a 24-point lead to one point with a little over two minutes to play.

"We still ended up losing (87-80). But in that game, Michael showed the ultimate in confidence and arrogance. I don't think anybody else would have kept trying after missing his first 14 shots the way he did. But he still found a way to get hot late in the game and come so close to pulling it out. That was the most amazing turnaround I've ever seen a player have."

ot hot

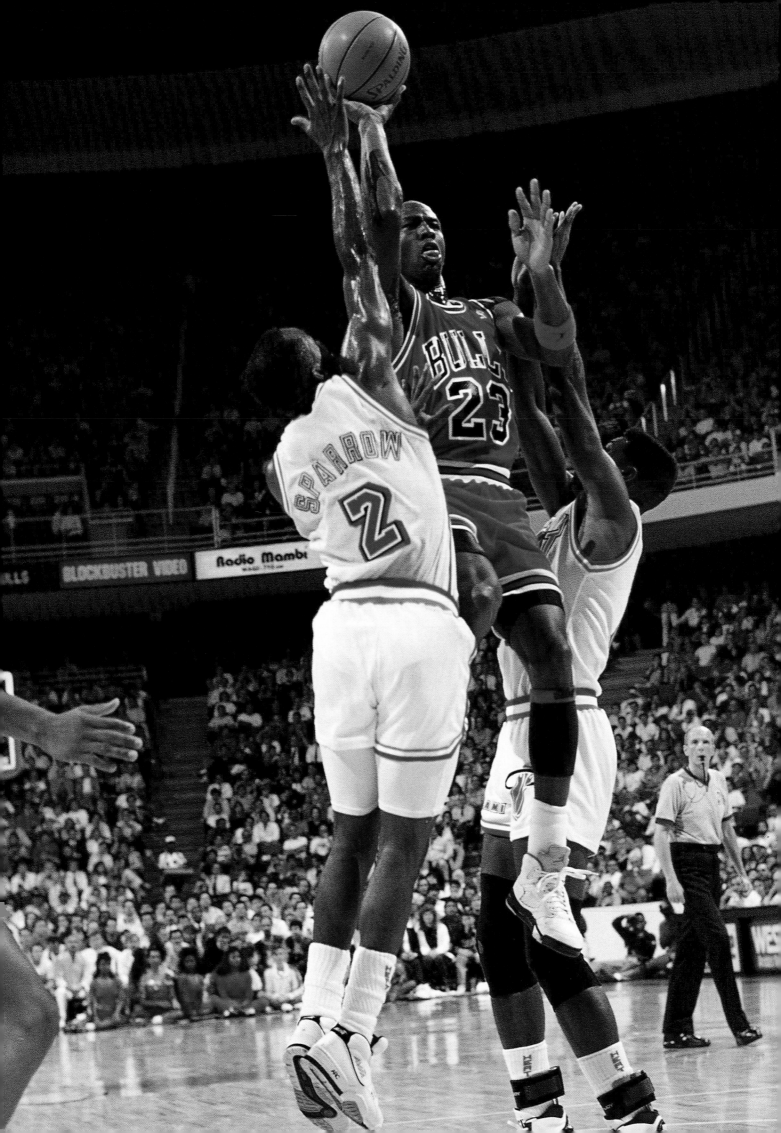

Steve Smith

Atlanta Hawks guard, on the third and final
game of the Miami/Chicago playoff series in 1992

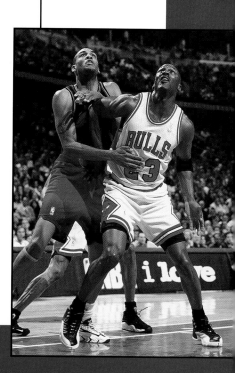

"During my rookie year with the Miami Heat, one of my teammates, Willie Burton, did something he shouldn't have done. When Jordan didn't score any points in the first quarter, Willie told Michael, 'Hey, we're shutting you down tonight. We're going to stop you.' Well, what did he want to do that for? Michael went on to score 56 points in the last three quarters. The worst thing about what Willie did was he was not the primary man guarding Michael. I was. So I have 56 unpleasant memories of Jordan from that playoff game."

George Karl

Seattle SuperSonics head coach after musing that Jordan had become a
jump shooter, then watching Mike go for 50 in a 1997 game in Seattle

"There's no way you can say, 'Defend him better.' We were there, he fades, he's in the crowd, we're near him and he hits them."

he hits them

Jeff Van Gundy

Knicks head coach, on how Jordan scored 20 in the fourth quarter as the Bulls rallied to win at Madison Square Garden in 1997

"A lot of people have asked that question. No answers yet. . . . (Double-teams) have to come from some angle. And whatever angle it comes from, he goes the other way. And he's able to beat two defenders, which is his greatness."

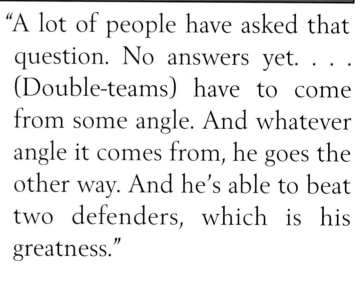

Larry Bird

"That's why he's the best player in the league.
That's why he's probably the greatest player ever."

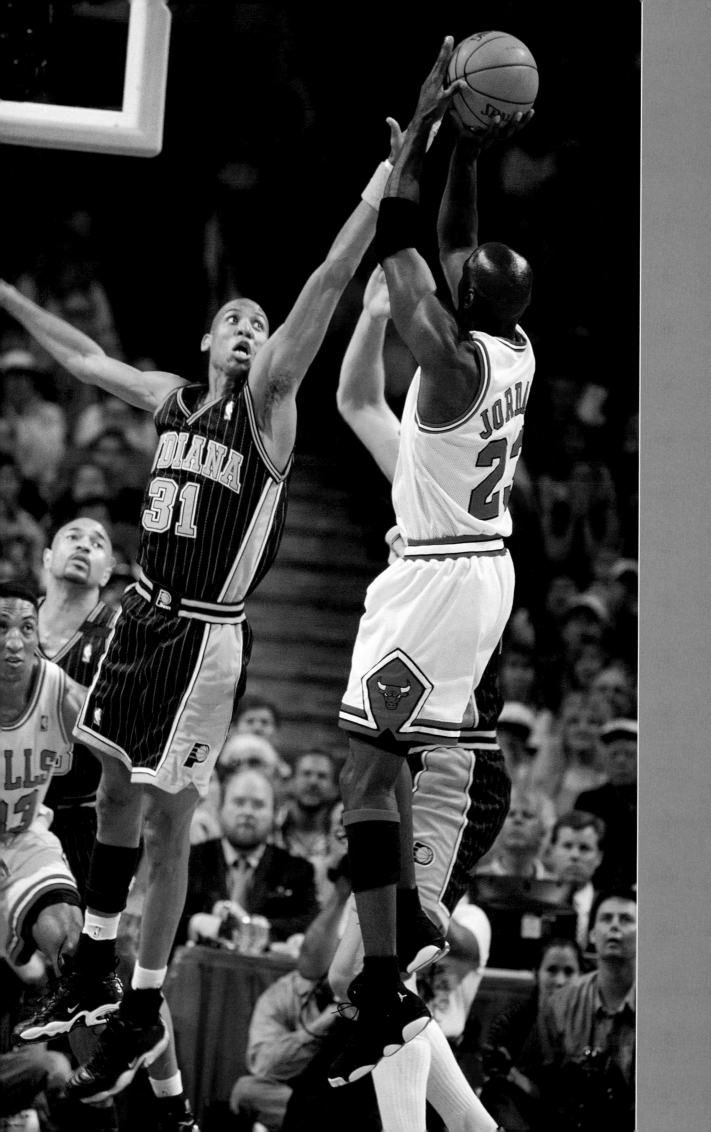

shocked us all

Mike Wise

NBA writer for The New York Times, on the final seconds of the last game of the 1998 Finals

"I remember Mike Wilbon of the Washington Post turning to me with about three minutes left in Game 6 of the Finals and saying, 'He's done. He has nothing left in his legs. I know this guy. I'm telling you, he's done.'

"Having written off Jordan a half-dozen times over the last few years, I nodded and started to craft my story that night in a way that made him sound old and beaten down. He had missed his last six shots, and the Bulls were spent in front of the loudest crowd of the season. When John Stockton nailed a three-pointer with about 41 seconds left, everything seemed to fall in place for a sportswriter trying to meet a deadline. All I had to do was plug the final score in and hit the send button on my computer.

"There was one problem: He wasn't done.

"In 36 surreal seconds, Michael stole the Jazz's soul and, well, the first eight paragraphs of my story. Of all the games I've covered, watching him poke the ball away (from Karl Malone) on one end and drop in the game-winning shot (over Bryon Russell) on the other was the most wild and dramatic sequence I can recall. Wilbon disappeared after his proclamation and I haven't seen him since. He's probably still shaking his head. The truth is, as well as any of us could know the guy, he shocked us all that night."

Refuse to Lose

There are some things that you just don't do in life. You don't send cash in the mail, especially to an attorney or the IRS.

You don't play leap-frog with a unicorn. You don't scream "Pee Wee" in a crowded theater.

And by all means, you never, ever make Michael Jordan mad on a basketball court. Or as his college roomie Buzz Peterson will tell you, better not make Michael Jordan mad – period.

Peterson remembers the time at North Carolina when he and Jordan played a friendly game of Monopoly. Well, one luxury tax led to another, and before he knew it, Jordan was flat out of luck. So he picked up a handful of play money, threw it in the air like confetti and stormed out of the room before it had fluttered to the floor. Hypercompetitive? It seems that Peterson has felt the wrath of Jordan every time the two have met on the golf course ever since.

By now, it's no secret that Jordan is the worst loser in the history of history. The guy absolutely hates to get beat, let alone embarrassed, and although that happens about as often as it snows in Winslow, Ariz., heaven help the person who pulls it off. Take the 1985 NBA All-Star Game in Indianapolis, for instance. Turned off by Jordan's gaudy dress at the events of the previous day, Isiah Thomas and a few other veteran players aimed to teach their rookie teammate a lesson in humility. So Thomas orchestrated a freeze-out of Jordan in the main event, a plan that he learned of afterward.

Here's another one: Don't dare ruffle Jordan's feathers when you are scheduled to play against him the very near future. Two nights later, the raging Bull promptly dropped 49 points on Thomas and the Pistons in an overtime victory.

You see, Jordan has this thing about payback. In February 1993, a Washington Bullet named LaBradford Smith had a career game at his expense, lit Jordan up for 37 points – in his own backyard, no less. In the return match at Landover, Md., the following night, Jordan informed Smith that he would have 37 points by halftime. Jordan lied. He had only 34 points at halftime and finished with 47.

Move to January 1996. Rookie Jerry Stackhouse announced that Jordan was overrated, that he had more than held his own when the former Tar Heels played one-on-one at North Carolina. Dumb-de-dumb-dumb. Hours later, Jordan answered with 48 biggies at Philadelphia, and he would have had more had the victory not been a 37-point blowout.

Say, does Saddam Hussein know about this guy?

Then there was the time exactly one year later when Jordan's favorite head coach, Jeff Van Gundy, called him a con man. According to the Knicks' boss, Jordan befriended the younger players in the league as a way to set them up for the kill later. Maybe the analysis was more truth than fiction, but he didn't much care. After Jordan torched the Knicks for 51 points at Madison Square Garden, he said to Van Gundy, "Con that, little guy." Or something like that, anyway.

Anyone try Scrabble lately?

Flip Saunders

Timberwolves head coach

"My favorite story — I don't know if you should print it — was in 1996. At our place, he and (point guard) Darrick Martin got into it. When we went to play them at their place a couple of weeks later, he wouldn't let (Martin) get the ball past half court.

"At one point, he said to Darrick, 'I'm going to put you back in the CBA.'

Well, I didn't start Darrick in the second half, and (Jordan) walked past our bench and said, 'I didn't know I'd do it in a half."

Kevin Garnett

Timberwolves forward

"I remember that game when he told Darrick Martin, 'You're a CBA player and you don't even belong in the game, 'cause you're a backup.' Any time people ask me about Mike, that's what I tell 'em about."

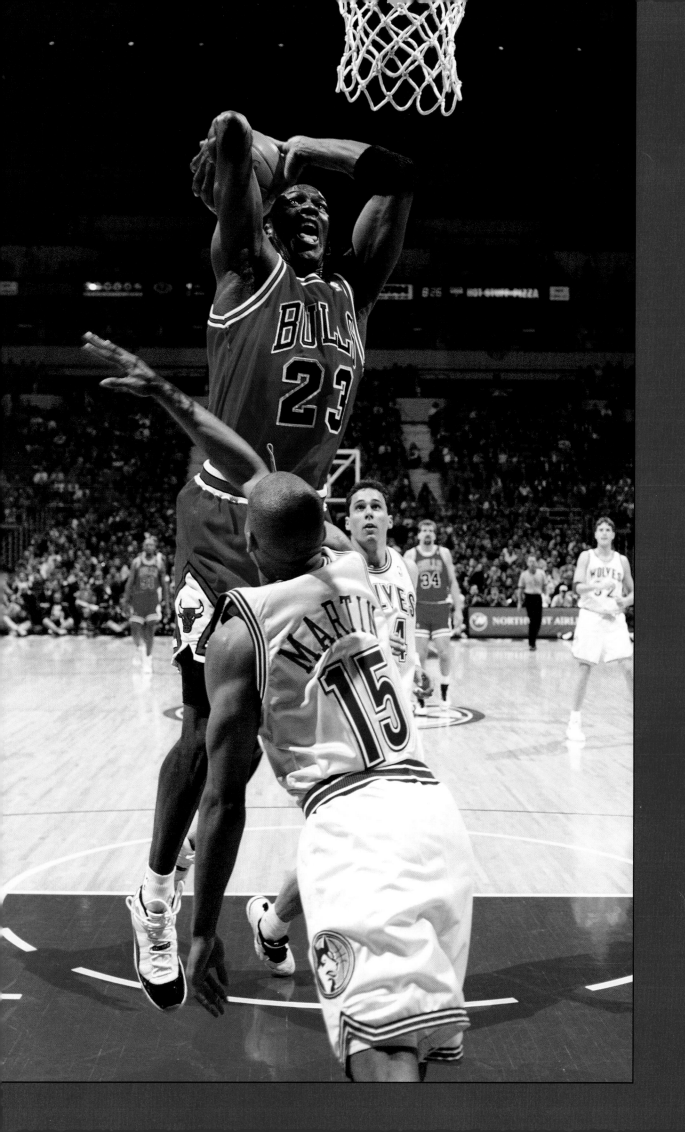

killer

Charles Barkley

"What do you think it is that allows him to have success like he has, where he wins championship after championship? You absolutely need that competitive nature in this game if you want to stay on top. Magic Johnson had it, Larry Bird had it, and Michael has it, too. To win a couple of championships, you have to have that killer instinct and competitive nature. And Michael has six (titles)."

"The way Michael approached training camp . . . he had something to prove (after coming back from retirement). Every day was a war out there and he set the tone right from the beginning, the first day of camp. I thought that was the reason we had such a great season because from day one it was established that we were going to get after it. And that meant from day one on the practice floor, too."

Steve Kerr

instinct

Sam Smith

NBA writer for the Chicago Tribune, author of "The Jordan Rules"

"It was really the beginning of their run, during the 1989 playoffs (against Cleveland). Now, this is when the Cavaliers are the up-and-coming team in the league, a team Magic Johnson called the future power in the East.

"Of the three beat writers covering (the Bulls), Lacy Banks picks them to lose to Cleveland in three games, Kent McDill picks them to lose in four games, and I pick them to lose in five. They split the first four games and go back to Cleveland for what would become one of Michael's signature moments (his last-second, game-winning shot over Craig Ehlo).

"Jordan walks up to me right before the game is about to start. He points to Lacy and says, 'We took care of you.' He points at Kent and says, 'We took care of you.' He then looks at me and says, 'Today, we take care of you.'"

power

embarrass you

John Starks

ex-Knicks guard

"Whenever you're playing against Michael he's going to bring out the best in you. You know what type of competitor he is, and you know he is the type of player who can embarrass you on any given night. So you have to bring your best game in order to play against him."

intense

Danny Ainge

Suns coach and a former MJ antagonist for the Celtics

"I always thought Larry (Bird) worked harder than anybody, getting the absolute most from his skills. And back then I never thought that Michael or anyone could ever be as intense as Larry in terms of winning. But Michael is at least his equal in all those categories, besides being the superior athlete."

determination

determination

determination

Jerry Sloan

Jazz head coach

"In the 1997 Finals, John Stockton had picked him clean on one end and began racing up court. Jordan had fallen down and was out of the play. A few seconds later, with Stockton driving the lane, Jordan knocked the ball away. He was so determined to get that ball back that he got up and sprinted down the court. You can't coach or teach that kind of determination."

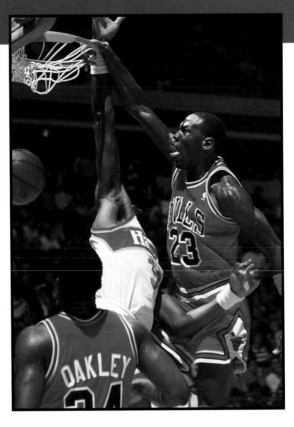

Larry Bird

Celtics great and Pacers head coach

"On a scale of one to 10, with the rest of the superstars an
eight, he's a 10 . . . I just hope there aren't any more of him
to come along that we have to deal with."

Isiah Thomas

Ex-Pistons great and current TV analyst

"During my career when I played against Michael, I found him to be the ultimate challenge because he was so fundamentally sound, so physically gifted and mentally tough that it was hard to break him down in any area. You'd marvel at the things that he did out on the court. But you could never let him know that you admired him because he'd see that as a sign of weakness and he'd devour you."

"He will abuse you and talk about you and hit shots in your face and tell you that you can't do this or that. Guys know every day when you come to that gym you're going to have to go hard. If you don't he will talk you to death."

Ron Harper

Bulls guard

Penny Hardaway

Magic guard

"I love playing against him. That's what this game is all about, going against someone like Michael Jordan. He brings out my best, and I'm sure the best in everyone he plays. You never have trouble getting ready to play him."

Nick Anderson

Magic guard and Chicago native

"I love the guy. You grow up idolizing him, then you get the chance to play against him. I'd love to play against him every night. He's what the game is all about. If you aren't ready to play, he'll kill you."

kicks their butts

Jeff Van Gundy

"You watch him, game in and game out and he sidles up next to guys and smiles at them, pats them on the butt and then he goes out there and kicks their butts. And they hug him after the game, like that was some great thing that he got 45 on them. I don't understand it. He sucks them into thinking that he wants to see them develop. He talks about young players, he invites people to be in his movies, and it's all a con."

CHAPTER 4

Invaluable Commodity

What has been Michael Jordan's worth to the NBA? Hmmmm. Let's see . . . take the fortunes of Bill Gates and Bud Walton, multiply them by the number of dye jobs Dennis Rodman has donned and then add six (for MJ's NBA titles) and you'll be about halfway to your answer. Simply put, Michael Jordan IS (or WAS) the NBA. Putting a price tag on his value is like trying to guard him . . . impossible.

A person can't go 15 minutes without a visual reminder of Jordan in some form, whether it be a billboard, a television commercial, a highlight film or on the shelf of a supermarket. From Peoria to Paris, Michael Jordan is without peer in name recognition. As executive NBA vice president Rick Welts says, "(Michael) has changed the public's view of what role athletes can play in society."

With more than a little help from the league, which knows the value of a Bull market when it sees one, Jordan has become a brand name unto himself.

What do you think about when you hear the name, Michael Jordan? In-your-face slam dunks? Sure. Game-winning three-pointers? Of course. A champion among champions? Indeed. But you also so readily associate his name with Coca-Cola, Gatorade, Nike, Hanes, Wheaties, Oakley, Rayovac and Upper Deck — his best-known endorsements — that you'd think MJ played his home games on Madison Avenue, not the United Center. What has been Michael Jordan's worth to the NBA? Put down the calculators and write down the sign for "infinity."

Why do you think that Michael's decision to retire upstaged President Clinton's impeachment trial? Because, like it or not, one man IS larger than an entire league. For the last five or so years, several million column inches have been written about which young star will step up to the challenge of replacing Jordan. Pretenders to the throne such as Harold "Baby Jordan" Miner, Jerry Stackhouse, Shaquille O'Neal and Penny Hardaway have not quite compelled fans to throw out their Jordan posters. Grant Hill certainly possesses the right attitude and a solid all-around game, but the fire to win hasn't shown itself as of yet. Kobe Bryant owns all the moves and actually resembles his idol right down to the postgame interview-speak. But this young man's game needs plenty of polish before fans and Madison Avenue are ready to anoint a new King.

What has been Michael's worth to the NBA? Some say he cannot be replaced and his departure will spell doom for the NBA. That's a bit drastic. After all, Babe Ruth retired and baseball managed to stay afloat. The NBA will survive and eventually thrive again without Michael Jordan. It just won't be as fun to watch, darn it.

Jayson Williams

New Jersey forward

"I call Michael Jordan 'Black Jesus.' I don't mean anything in that. It's just that he is some sort of basketball god who is able to do whatever he wants to. He is absolutely that best player to ever play the game. And if there's one thing I tell my teammates, it's not to make Black Jesus mad.

"Michael can talk all the trash he wants to for two reasons. First, he's earned the right to do so because of how long he has been playing and all the things that he has accomplished. Second, because he can back it up with his game. He has the rings. So until we get what he's got, it's best for us to keep our mouths shut and just keep working hard and improving. Then one day, when we get rings, we can talk back to people like Michael."

Dick Ebersol

president of NBC Sports

"Michael, probably more than any other athlete in any sport, is a great draw for the casual fan. People that don't care much about basketball still care about seeing Michael Jordan."

Scott Williams

former Bulls teammate

"People who don't know anything about basketball know about Michael Jordan. He's really the only household name in the game."

Larry King

TV/radio interview host

"What Michael means to the city of Chicago cannot be put into words. He is the city. He personifies the best of Chicago and he is its largest sports hero ever. I thought for years that there would never be one bigger than Ernie Banks, or George Halas' old Chicago Bears and their great legends. He has transcended them all."

Ray Meyer

former DePaul head coach

"He brings so much enjoyment not only to the people who watch him in person, but he brings excitement to all walks of life. He brings entertainment to the elderly, the sick, the shut-ins and kids of all ages. When it comes to sports in Chicago, he is THE topic of conversation."

best of Chicago

changed the game

Scottie Pippen

ex-Chicago forward

"We've used each other in a way, had an impact that changed the whole game. We've always tried to come out and be dominant. He's one of the greatest scorers of all time. I've tried to be one of the greatest all-around players of all time. We've been able to feed off each other, and enjoy the success we've had together."

Larry Brown

Philadelphia 76ers head coach

"He's simply the best player, the best team player in any team sport I've ever seen. No one will ever replace Michael. I look at Larry (Bird), Magic (Johnson), Julius (Erving), (Karl) Malone, Hakeem Olajuwon. All of these guys were phenomenal, but Michael is something different."

team player

Dave Checketts

Madison Square Garden president

"When I first got here, when John MacLeod was the (Knicks') coach and Jordan was sweeping us in three, I was humiliated. I wanted to beat him so badly. But in my later years, the rage turned into respect for what he's accomplished. You can't help but admire his sheer will. Much as he's been our adversary, Jordan's been great for us. Every time he comes to the Garden he puts on a show."

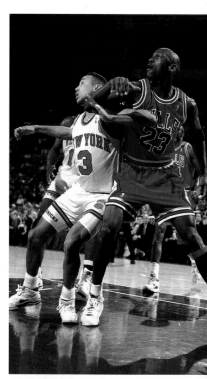

puts on a show

Pat Riley

Miami Heat head coach

"I don't think anyone is going to win until Michael retires. This is one of the dilemmas of a lot of good teams – the Knicks for instance. Sometimes you can build a great team that could be a championship team, but you never win because you have the misfortune of being there when Jordan is going through his run. I saw that when we had Magic, Kareem [Abdul-Jabbar] and [James] Worthy, when there were some very good teams in the Western Conference that probably could have won. It's unfortunate that some teams that are good have to wait right now because this team is great. By the time [the Bulls] get old, that team is old, too."

financial

Charles Barkley

Houston Rockets forward

"He's made all of us a lot of money. The three greatest influences in pro basketball, as far as financial rewards for everybody are concerned, have been Magic Johnson, Larry Bird and Michael Jordan. Magic and Bird started it. And Michael took it to another level. For the sake of finances and for the sake of us now getting great exposure all around the world, we should all be grateful to Michael."

ewards

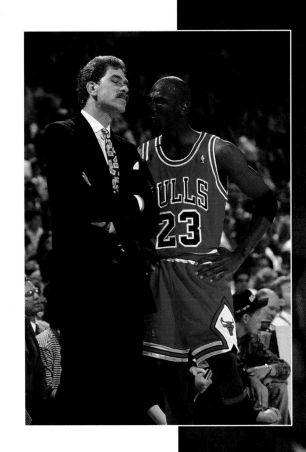

Magic Johnson

Los Angeles Lakers great

"But Michael – we need you one more year. Michael, please don't go. The league needs you and these players sure need you. And I need you, too, as a fan because I'll tell you the truth: I don't know how much basketball I'd even want to watch without Michael. You see — Michael, Phil Jackson and Pat Riley and very few others understand the real beauty of five guys playing the game together. They understand how to compete and get guys going. So I can't see the league without Michael because we are not ready and there's

David Stern

"What I will say is that no one will ever replace Michael Jordan. He is the most famous athlete of his time and perhaps with Muhammad Ali, of any time. When he retires, there is going to be a void that no one player can fill. We will see Shaquille O'Neal, Penny Hardaway, Kevin Garnett, Grant Hill, a long list of players will step up. I don't think it will be quite the same circumstance when Michael Jordan came along.

"The Nikes and Reeboks and Filas did not do the kind of advertising they do now. The relationship with the McDonald's and Cokes in sports was not as big. And the television, cable and satellite delivery hadn't even begun to develop. There will never be a growth spurt like that again."

going to be a void

CHAPTER 5

Reflections of Greatness

It's easy to take a quick glance at Michael Jordan's life and say, "Sign me up!" After all, who wouldn't want to be the greatest basketball player, the richest spokesman and coolest cat in all the land?

But life in the penthouse – or in this case, the largest goldfish bowl on the planet – isn't always what it's cracked up to be.

Just ask any member of Mike's security force. Through his final season of 1997-98, his bodyguards received more bumps and bruises following a 10-second walk from the team bus to the hotel lobby than Dennis Rodman delivers to Anthony Mason in 48 minutes on the hardwood.

No matter what the city, state or country, a Michael Jordan sighting incites some pretty weird stuff.

Although he's considered royalty around the world – he's the most popular athlete since Muhammad Ali – Jordan's subjects often treat His Airness like a rock star, not a king. Everyone wants a piece of the living legend . . . and often, these people will go to dangerous lengths to get it. Several years ago in Los Angeles, one die-hard Jordan fanatic actually laid down in front of the team bus and refused to move until his wish to speak with his idol was granted. It took awhile, but the guy finally became convinced that impersonating a speed bump was not for him.

The insanity reached new heights in Washington, D.C., two seasons ago when Jordan found himself and his teammates in the scariest situation imaginable. A large posse of fans had camped out at the team hotel since late morning, and when it came time for the

defending champions to board their bus to the arena hours later, word spread like wildfire. It wasn't long before Jordan and company were engulfed by dozens of giddy star-gazers who serenaded them with chants of "Mich-ael!," "Scot-tie!," "Mich-ael!," "Den-nis!," "Mich-ael!"

While this scene had become commonplace, there was one important difference. Unlike the curb-side service that's routine at the other stops on the NBA tour, team members were required to travel a distance of nearly 150 feet to the bus door. Worse yet, there were precious few security personnel to protect the players. Talk about the running of the Bulls. As team media services director Tom Smithberg recalls, "That was as scared as I ever had seen (the team). And that includes Michael."

1 NCAA championship • 2 Olympic gold medals • 3 NBA steals titles • 5 NBA MVP awards
6 Finals MVP awards • 6 NBA championships • 10 NBA scoring titles
11 All-Star games • 31.5 Career scoring average • 33.4 Career playoffs scoring average
63 Playoffs scoring high • 69 Regular season scoring high • 29,277 Total points, third all-time

Julius Erving

NBA Hall of Famer and vice president of Orlando Magic

"I didn't have that type of pressure weighing on me. I did not have that type of role or responsibility in my twilight years. I had Magic Johnson, Larry Bird, Michael, Karl Malone, John Stockton, Kevin McHale and a host of other good players and solid citizens coming along after me. These are guys destined to make the transition from athlete to non-athlete and still be a great credit to the sport, society and themselves. I could go and not feel guilty about leaving the league hanging. But he has to deal with that."

pressure

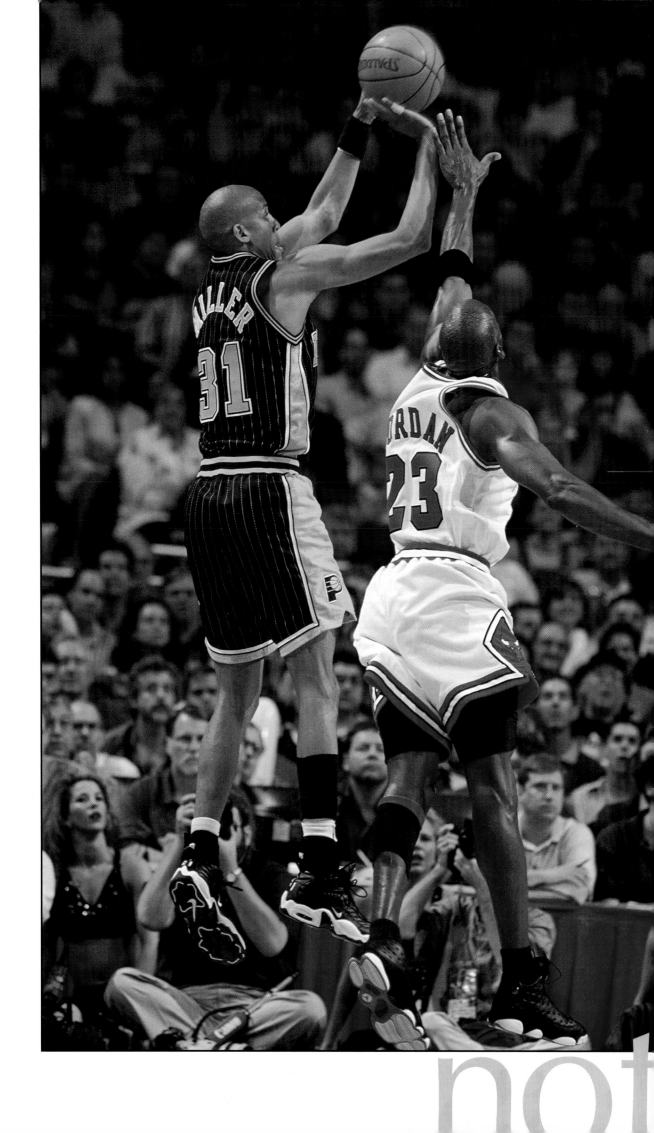

not

"Are you of this Earth?"
Jordan:
"Well, I come from Chicago."

Reggie Miller

Indiana Pacers guard

"The guy keeps going when everyone else around him stops. I am telling you, he's not human. Has anyone ever seen him bleed? I have not seen blood yet. Something is going on here. He is not human."

human

Anfernee Hardaway

Orlando Magic guard

"Michael Jordan is 'Da man.' He is. He took the torch from Larry Bird and Isiah Thomas and those guys when they retired and he just took over. He's an ambassador on and off the floor. His basketball talent speaks for itself. But his business mind is now coming to the top and that puts him on a higher level than any other guys in the league."

Shaquille O'Neal

has set the standard for all of us, in so many ways. On the court. Off the court. What can I say? He's a great player. t more importantly, he's a great winner. I think that's what people will measure him by when he leaves."

Jack Ramsay

Former head coach of the Portland Trail Blazers, the team that passed on Jordan for Sam Bowie

"We had Jim Paxson and Clyde Drexler at shooting guard and that wasn't bad at all because Paxson was an All-Star and Clyde was a future All-Star. So we didn't need help at shooting guard. We needed a center. We were hoping to draft Hakeem Olajuwon until we lost the coin flip. Nobody, and I mean nobody, knew that Michael would develop into the player he would become. Had we known, who knows? I guess what we should have done was trade Paxson and Drexler and taken Michael. But it's easy to look back in hindsight. Remember, Michael didn't win a title until his seventh year."

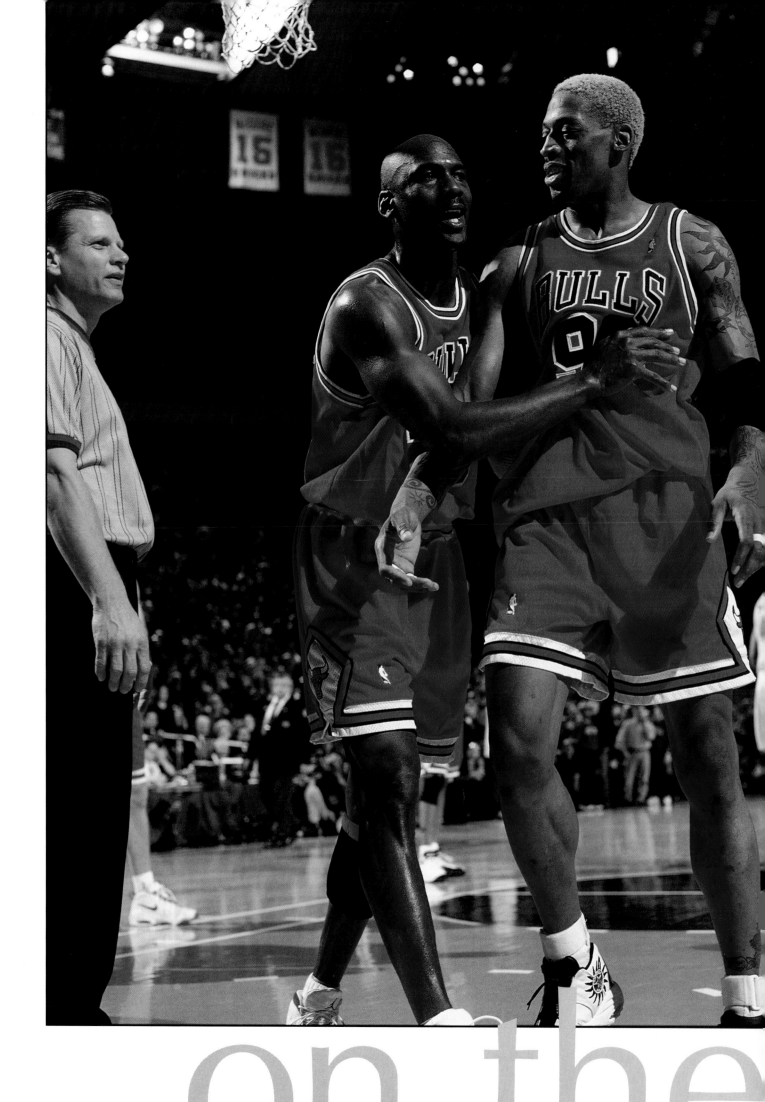

on the

Dennis Rodman

ex-Chicago Bulls power forward

"Michael Jordan is the only superstar in the game who comes through every time. Anyone next to him just pales."

"People say, 'When did you know who he was?' We knew in the first practice. Kevin (Loughery) and I just looked at one another, shook our heads. We had seen Earl Monroe, Elgin Baylor, Jerry West. We couldn't believe what we were seeing. If you think you can just create another title (without him), you're sitting in the wrong pew. Michael's sitting on the altar."

Fred Carter

Former coach with the Chicago Bulls

altar

Karl Malone

Utah Jazz power forward

"The greatest thing about me winning the MVP (award in 1996-97) was the fact that I beat out Michael Jordan to win it. Either of us deserved it, but I was happy that I could at least win one of those awards. After all, Michael had already won four. I respect Michael because I believe he is the best player to ever play the game."

Lenny Wilkens

Hall of Famer, NBA head coach

"Obviously, I've played and coached against the greatest players ever and Michael Jordan is simply the greatest because of his athleticism, his matchless skills and his tremendous mental toughness."

Jerry West

Hall of Famer, Lakers operations chief

"I think you almost forget about his greatness because he seems to perform at that level all the time. The extraordinary becomes the ordinary for him."

Magic Johnson

Los Angeles Lakers great

"My best skill was controlling the team and winning. He's a better scorer, has better everything than I had. Larry (Bird) has said it. We have always said that, both of us. When you know that you're good, you don't have a problem giving it up for somebody else. We both know we dominated in our time. But you ask, were we as good as Michael Jordan? No. He does a little bit more – does this, does this, does this, better than both of us, and we understand that. We did what we had to do. Nobody can take away his (Bird's) three championships, my five championships, but we're not sitting here thinking that we were better than Michael Jordan."

higher

Julius Erving

NBA Hall of Famer and vice president of Orlando Magic

"There is a lot in common with us – the ability to create, to play team ball, but when that breaks down, be able to take over a game and create at a higher level than many of your peers. I think that brings about a certain type of respect, a reverence. But once you acquire that role – like we did – you have to measure up, to stand up to it every night, to do the same things over and over again. I was able to do it in my 16 years, and certainly I've seen Michael do it at an even higher level during his 13 years.

"The better player? When I was 26, nobody was better than I was. Between 26-30 is when I was at my best. Him at 26 versus me at 26? I don't know. I can't fathom being second to anyone at that stage, but I'm sure he can't either."

evel

Jimmy "Jam" Harris

Grammy Award-winning music producer

"Michael already was shaping up as the best player of all time. But he turned that up to become the ultimate player for a team. I equate it very much to music. It's a passion that you have. He's someone who wants to play basketball all the time. He's not doing it for the money. It's appropriate that he's the highest paid player, because with him, it never was about the money. You could never pay him enough money.

"Music is a God-given talent. If you're passionate about it, you're going to do it no matter what. With him, he'd be playing basketball whether he's getting paid or not.

"Michael's a riveting guy. When he speaks, you hang on every word. But he's also a very intense listener. He asked me some music questions, and I could tell by his follow-up questions that he really wanted to know what was up. That's his intensity. He's a well-studied guy. Whether it's a clothing line or cologne or basketball. He always does his homework."

assionate

Mitch Richmond

Washington Wizards veteran guard

"Michael has often said that I remind him of himself and to me that is the ulti   mate compliment. Maybe the greatest favor anybody ever did for me was when he gave up his spot on the second Dream Team because he said he wanted me to replace him and get a shot at a gold medal. That showed the tremendous human side of MJ. It showed he's not just a great player but a great person. I'll always be grateful to him for that . . . I've always enjoyed   playing against him. (But) I just know I saw the bottom of his shoes a lot over the years."

David Falk

Jordan's agent and the man who coined "Air Jordan"

"He's just a very, very, very special guy."

Kevin Loughery

"We thought he was going to be good, or we don't take him third in the draft. We also thought he was a franchise player. But never could we have fathomed he was gonna be the best player ever to play. But when we put in one-on-one drills the third day, we saw he had the ability to take the ball anyplace on the floor that he wanted to take it, and that he could do things that shocked us.

"Then about two weeks into the camp, you find out he was about as great a competitor as you're gonna find. And then, you know, the guy walks in the gym the first day as a rookie coming out of college early, and he's the leader immediately — so he had the whole package."

Bill Fitch

Houston head coach when the Rockets drafted Hakeem Olajuwon No. 1

"I remember (UNC head coach Dean Smith) saying to me, 'It must be tough passing up the surest-fire All-Star ever to come into the game. Dean knew then. People knock him as the only one who could hold Jordan to fewer than 20 points a game, but his system had a lot to do with him becoming the player he did. He didn't do too bad for himself after he left North Carolina, did he?"

rookie

George Mikan

"He's perfected the game in so many areas. We had guys like Elgin Baylor and Jimmy Pollard, who had that great leaping ability. But they never reached the pinnacle that he has. He's so exciting. He's good for the game."

Bill Russell

've watched you play hundreds of times and every night you play like Michael Jordan . . . I've never een a game where you sent your shoes or your uniform out there and took the night off. The thing really, really enjoy, (is when) you see games where things are not going exactly the way you want them to go and (I can) watch you figure out how to win this game. I guess the reason I enjoy hem so much is because I felt I went through the ame kinds of things. I feel like you're a soul mate."

David Stern

NBA commissioner at Jordan's
retirement news conference

"This is not a sad day. This is a great day, because the greatest basketball player in the history of the game is getting the opportunity to retire with the grace that described his play."

Jordan

upon announcing his retirement

entally, I'm exhausted and I don't feel I have a challenge. It's sad that I'm leaving, but it's py because my life is starting to go into a whole other stage. I know, from a career stand-nt, I've accomplished everything I could as an individual.

ried to enhance the game itself, and I've tried to be the best basketball player I could be."

The Last Shot

June 14, 1998 Game 6 NBA Finals

Photographers

Photography by NBA Photos:

Bill Baptist

Andrew D. Bernstein

Nathaniel S. Butler

Lou Capozzola

Scott Cunningham

Gary Dineen

Garrett Ellwood

Sam Forencich

Barry Gossage

John Greishop

Andy Hayt

Ron Hoskins

Walter Iooss Jr. (and Sports Illustrated)

Mitchell Layton

Neil Leifer

Fernando Medina

Peter Read Miller

Bill Smith

Noren Trotman

Additional photography by

Brian Bahr/Allsport USA

Nathaniel Butler/Allsport USA

Jonathan Daniel/Allsport USA

Ann Heisenfelt Stringer/AP Wide World Photos

Brian Spurlock

Matthew Stockman/Allsport USA

UPI/Corbis-Bettman

Rocky Widner

Contributors

Writers

Paul Ladewski, who covered Jordan's entire NBA career as Bulls beat writer for the Daily Southtown Economist, wrote the chapter introductions.

Steve Aschburner, who covers the Minnesota Timberwolves for the Star Tribune Newspaper of the Twin Cities.

Lacy Banks, national NBA writer for the Chicago Sun-Times.

Mark Heisler, national NBA writer for the Los Angeles Times.

Tim Povtak, national NBA writer for the Orlando Sentinel.

Mike Wise, national NBA writer for The New York Times.